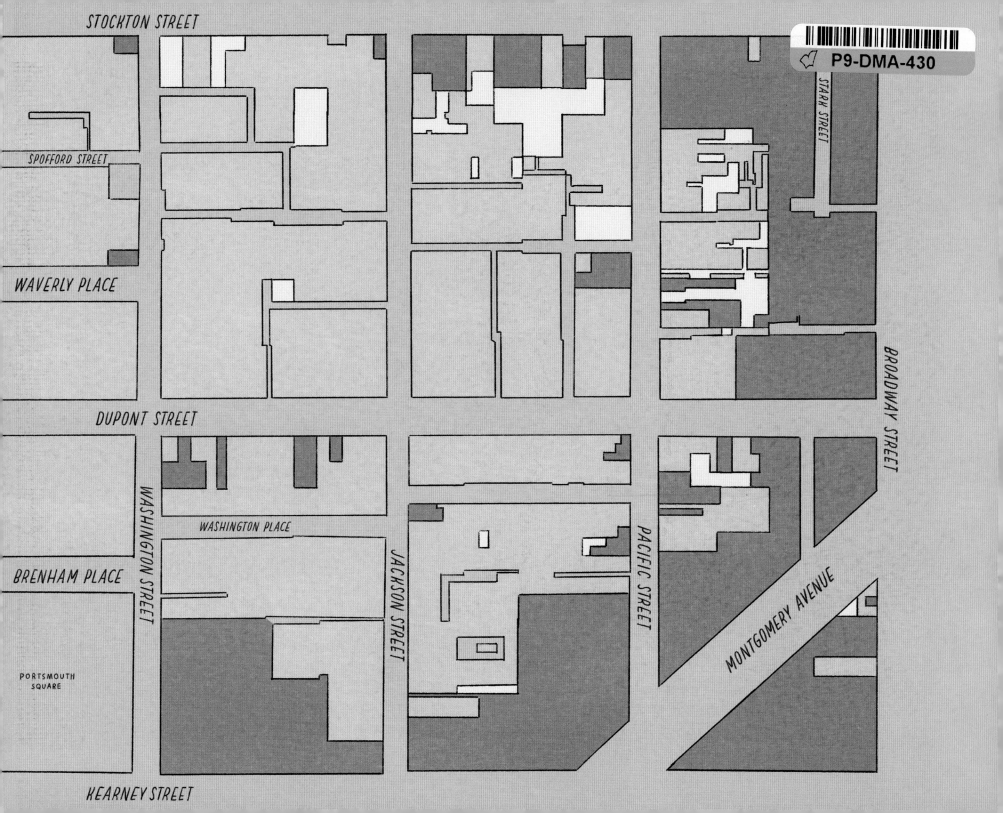

STOCKTON STREET

SPOFFORD STREET

WAVERLY PLACE

DUPONT STREET

WASHINGTON PLACE

BRENHAM PLACE

PORTSMOUTH SQUARE

WASHINGTON STREET

JACKSON STREET

PACIFIC STREET

STARK STREET

BROADWAY STREET

MONTGOMERY AVENUE

KEARNEY STREET

To the Dreamers, and to my niece Charlotte, a history ace.
—MB

*Special thanks to Sandra Wong for speaking
to me about her great-grandfather.*
—GL

ABOUT THIS BOOK

The illustrations for this book were done digitally in Adobe Photoshop. This book was edited by Alvina Ling and designed by Véronique Lefèvre Sweet. The production was supervised by Lillian Sun, and the production editor was Annie McDonnell. The text was set in 1906 French News, and the display type is the artist's hand lettering on the front cover and title page, and Avenir elsewhere.

I AM AN AMERICAN

The
WONG KIM ARK
★ ★ ★ Story ★ ★ ★

★ written by MARTHA BROCKENBROUGH with GRACE LIN ★

★ illustrated by JULIA KUO ★

Little, Brown and Company
New York Boston

Long ago, a boy was born in an apartment above a shop in San Francisco.

His name was Wong Kim Ark—and he believed something that would change this country.

I am an American.

m Kim Ark's apartment, he could
he clang of San Francisco's brand-
able car.

could smell the mouthwatering food
inatown's many restaurants.

could stand on his street and look
at San Francisco Bay, which opened
Pacific Ocean, which stretched all
ay to China, where his parents had
born.

Kim Ark's street had two names: Sacramento Street, after the state capital, and China Street, for the many people with Chinese ancestry who lived there.

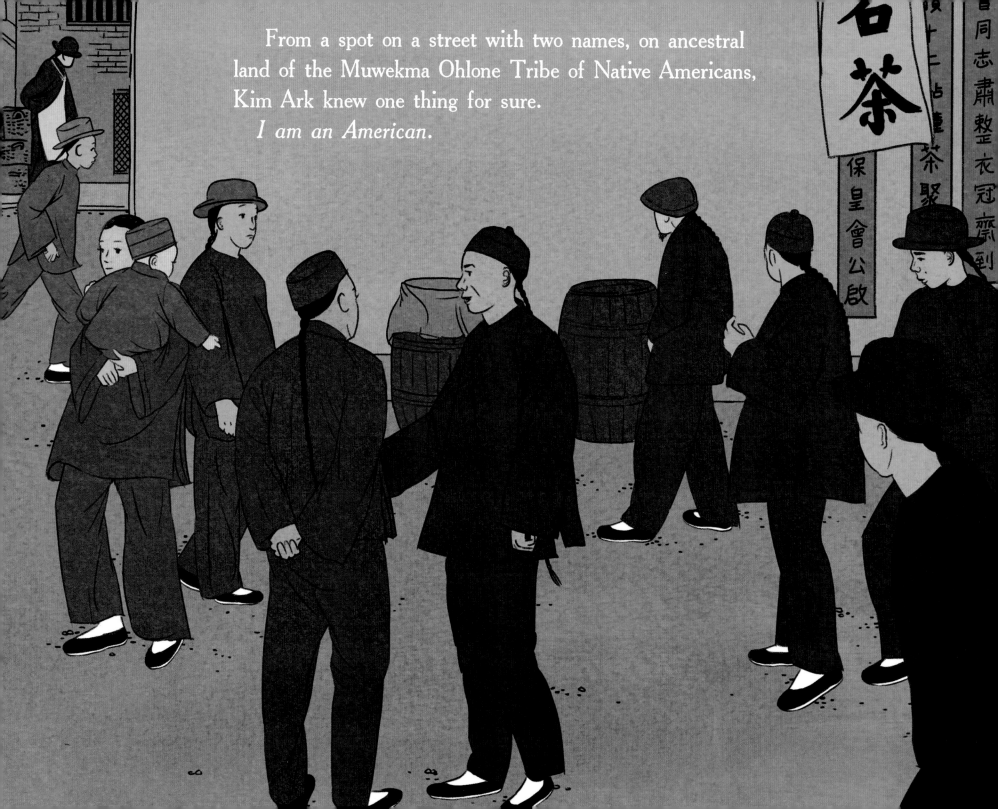

From a spot on a street with two names, on ancestral
land of the Muwekma Ohlone Tribe of Native Americans,
Kim Ark knew one thing for sure.
I am an American.

Many Chinese people like his parents had crossed
the ocean dreaming of a better life on Gold Mountain.
That's what Chinese people called California after
miners there struck it rich.
Some immigrants set up shops.

Some became farmers.
Some helped build a railroad stretching
from sea to sea, working hard for little money.

When Kim Ark was growing up, hard financial times hit. Many people blamed the Chinese.

They said people of Chinese heritage could *never* be American.

Kim Ark knew this was not true.

I am an American.

Even so, the country soon passed a law that said Chinese
workers could no longer come to the United States.
The law meant his parents could never be US citizens.
It meant Chinese people couldn't have certain jobs.
They couldn't live where they wanted.

And some people were cruel to Chinese Americans.
It became so hard to live in America that many decided to leave,
including Kim Ark's mom and dad.

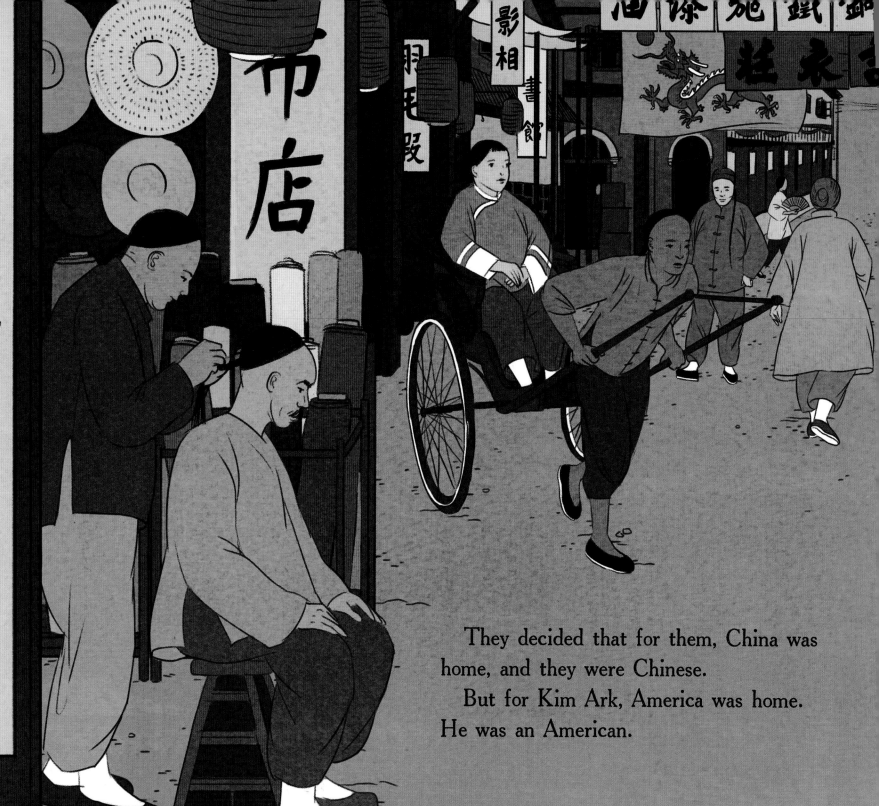

They decided that for them, China was
home, and they were Chinese.
But for Kim Ark, America was home.
He was an American.

He'd never even *been* to China until he visited his parents there after they moved.

After he returned to California,
he lived with his aunt and uncle
and worked as a cook.

He was only seventeen. He missed his family.
Kim Ark knew he might never see them again.
But he knew his job in America paid more, which
meant a better future.

Strict new laws meant he might not be allowed
back in the United States if he traveled to China.
A few years later, he decided to take the risk.

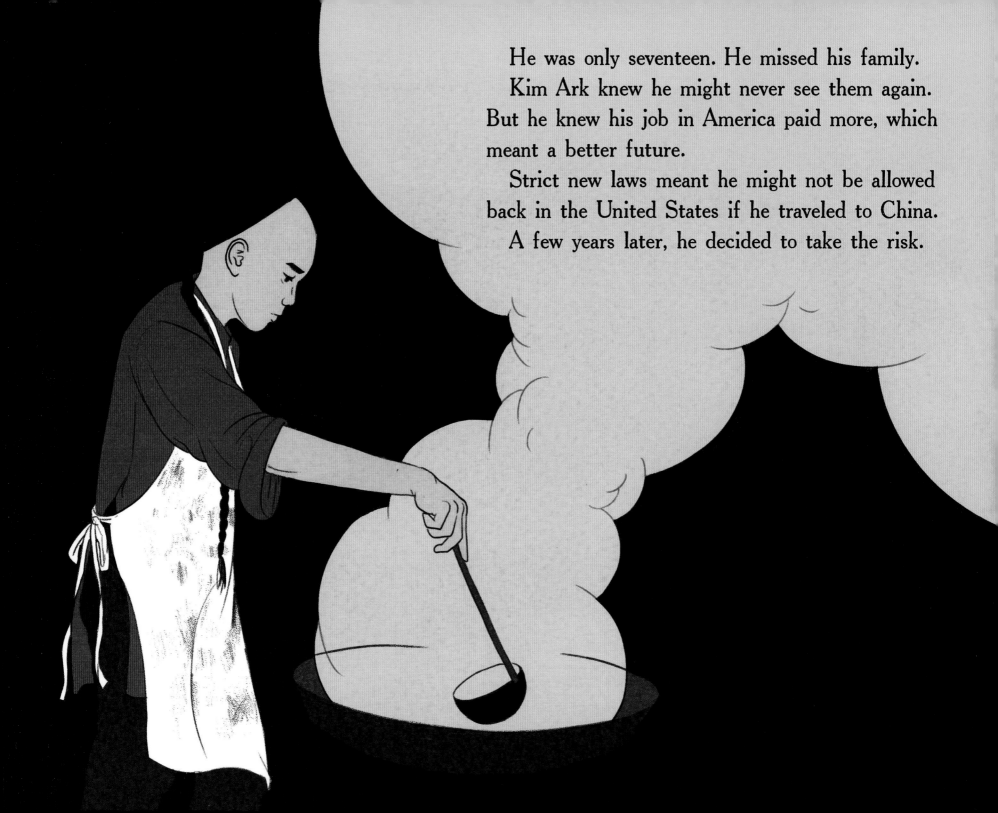

A law required him to find three white witnesses to sign a document swearing Kim Ark was born in California, that he was an American. He attached his picture to prove he was the young man in the letter.

He set sail once more for China. When he returned home
to San Francisco, he showed a customs official his papers.
"You are sure you were born here?" the official asked.
"Yes," Kim Ark said.
I am an American.
It didn't matter.

Authorities locked Kim Ark below deck, where it was cold, dark, and crowded.

He was moved from ship to ship and was imprisoned for more than four months.

Other people believed Wong Kim Ark. With their help, he won a lawsuit in San Francisco and was freed from the ship.

But the United States government wouldn't let him be.

Wong Kim Ark's case went all the way to the highest court in the land. The justices needed to decide an important question:

What makes someone American?

They looked to the US Constitution.

A part of it, the Fourteenth Amendment, says anyone born in America is a citizen.

But government lawyers said the Constitution didn't matter...that Kim Ark *couldn't* be a citizen because his Chinese ancestors had different customs and language from most people in America.

Kim Ark's fate depended on whom the justices believed.

And it wasn't only *his* future at stake.

Anyone with parents born elsewhere could also lose their right to call America theirs. So could citizens of Indigenous nations.

Kim Ark knew what he believed.

I am an American.

The Supreme Court justices pondered for almost a year.

Kim Ark waited. He worked. He worried. And then...

He won.

On March 28, 1898, six justices agreed that because he was born here, he belonged here. Kim Ark had known it all along. *I am an American.*

His victory changed the nation.

But the decision did not mean the end of unfair treatment of Chinese people and other minorities. For many people, America was often far from fair.

But Kim Ark's victory means that today, every child born in
the United States and its territories is an American, too...
no matter what language your parents speak,
what you look like,
or what you believe about God.

If you're born in the United States or its territories, you belong here, and it's your right to call yourself American. It's your right to call this home.
Always.

More About the Story

Even after Wong Kim Ark won his Supreme Court case, he and other people of Chinese ancestry continued to experience unfair treatment.

He always had to carry a certificate of identity with him to prove he was American. After a marriage in China was arranged for him and he became a father, one of his sons was not permitted entry from China. American officials didn't believe their relationship was valid. Three more sons did come to the United States. His son Wong Yook Jim spent weeks detained at Angel Island, an immigration station so dark, crowded, and miserable that detainees wrote and carved their sorrows on the walls in the form of poetry. Another son served in the US military. He was drafted into World War II and afterward served in the merchant marine. Today, Kim Ark has great-grandchildren in the United States.

Identification photograph on affidavit "In the Matter of Wong Kim Ark, Native Born Citizen of the United States" filed with the Immigration Service in San Francisco (*National Archives, Identifier 296479*)

The Fourteenth Amendment

The Fourteenth Amendment was ratified on July 9, 1868. Written after the Civil War, it was one of the Constitutional amendments meant to give citizenship and legal rights to people who had been enslaved.

First Chinese immigrants arrive.	Chinese Presbyterian Mission Church, the first Asian church in nation, opens.	Chinese Presbyterian Mission Church founds first school in nation for Chinese students.	California public schools bar students of color.	Chinese Presbyterian Mission School ends operations.	Wong Kim Ark born; Clay Street Cable Car begins running.
1849	1853	1859	1860	1871	1873

The first section of the Fourteenth Amendment states: "All persons born or naturalized in the United States, and subject to the jurisdiction thereof, are citizens of the United States and of the State wherein they reside."

How can a person become a US citizen?

Generally, at the time of this writing, you can be a US citizen if you were born here, or if at least one parent is a citizen. If only one of your parents is a citizen, you are a citizen if they live here and have custody of you. A citizen can also be naturalized, which means you have been granted citizenship even though you were born elsewhere. If one or more of your parents is naturalized, you gain citizenship

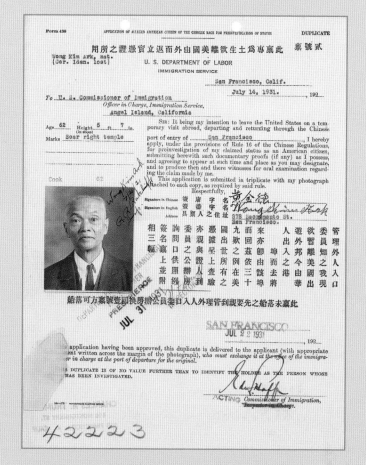

Application of Alleged American Citizen of the Chinese Race for Preinvestigation of Status by Wong Kim Ark
(National Archives, Identifier 18556185)

1874	1877	1878	1882
Black and Native American students granted segregated schools.	Riot in San Francisco targeting Chinese immigrants and their businesses. In two days of violence, four people died and more than $100,000 of Chinese-owned property was destroyed. (That would be worth more than $2.4 million today.)	Petition filed on behalf of three thousand Chinese American students for a public school.	Chinese Exclusion Act bars immigration of Chinese laborers for ten years.

automatically if you are a child and are a lawful permanent resident (have a green card) and live with that parent when they are naturalized.

Arguing against Wong Kim Ark

United States District Attorney Henry Foote argued against Wong Kim Ark in a lower court. Foote argued that "birth alone does not constitute right to citizenship in the United States" and that children born in the United States were "at the moment of birth, subject to a foreign power."

Foote was joined by George D. Collins, a San Francisco lawyer who wrote in the *American Law Review* that American-born Chinese people were culturally the same as people born in China. He believed this made them "unfit" to be American citizens. He later lost his law license and went to jail for being married to more than one woman and lying about it.

Holmes Conrad, a solicitor general for the Justice Department, was a Confederate cavalry officer during the Civil War. He argued at the Supreme Court level that states should determine citizenship, not the federal government. He also thought citizenship should be determined by shared culture and not birthplace, and he thought people of Chinese heritage could not assimilate into white American culture.

Arguing for Wong Kim Ark

Thomas Riordan defended the rights of people of Chinese ancestry in San Francisco and challenged

An eight-year-old girl named Mamie Tape sues and wins the right to attend a segregated public school.	Wong Kim Ark travels to China with his parents, Wong Si Ping and Wee Lee; Wong Kim Ark returns alone to San Francisco.	Geary Act requires registration of people of Chinese ancestry; people also must carry papers or face deportation.	Wong Kim Ark sails to China.	Wong Kim Ark detained in San Francisco.	Wong Kim Ark wins district court case and is released from ship.
1885	1890	1892	November 1894	August 1895	January 1896

other racist laws in court. He fought two other cases all the way to the Supreme Court.

Maxwell Evarts, a former US Assistant Attorney General, worked for Southern Pacific Railroad, which depended on Chinese workers.

J. Hubley Ashton was an international law expert who argued that the Fourteenth Amendment's wording meant birthright citizenship had to include people of Chinese descent born in the United States.

An association called the Chinese Consolidated Benevolent Association, sometimes called the Chinese Six Companies, worked on behalf of Chinese people in the United States. They helped settle conflicts among Chinese American people, and provided health services, education, and legal support in cases like Wong Kim Ark's.

Chinese store, Sacramento Street, San Francisco.

Acknowledgments

Thanks to Dean Gloster and Martin Lawler for advice on points of immigration law. Thanks also to Professor Erika Lee for sharing her deep knowledge of Wong Kim Ark and the Chinese American story.

United States v. Wong Kim Ark case argued in Supreme Court.	Supreme Court victory in *United States v. Wong Kim Ark*.	Chinese Exclusion Act made permanent.	Chinese Exclusion Act lifted; quotas limit immigration.	Wong Kim Ark dies in China, where he returned after continuing to experience discrimination in the United States.	Immigration and Naturalization Act abolishes quotas and sets up immigration policies designed to reunite families and attract skilled workers.
1897	1898	1902	1943	After World War II	1965

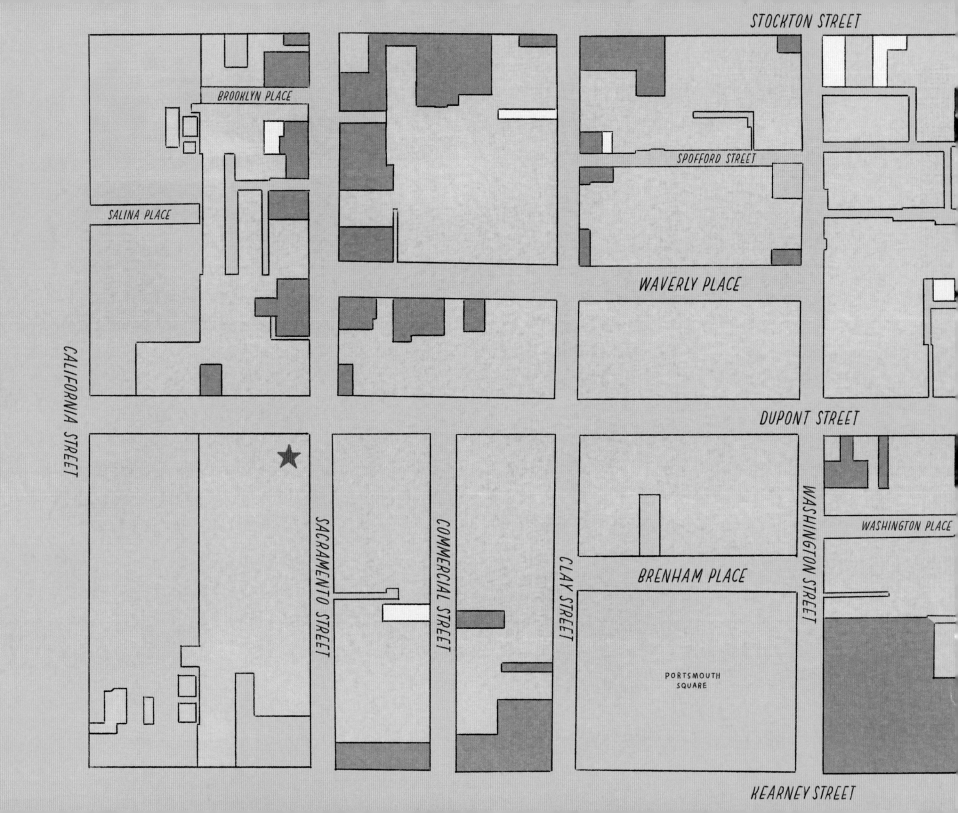

STOCKTON STREET

BROOKLYN PLACE

SALINA PLACE

SPOFFORD STREET

WAVERLY PLACE

CALIFORNIA STREET

DUPONT STREET

SACRAMENTO STREET

COMMERCIAL STREET

CLAY STREET

BRENHAM PLACE

WASHINGTON STREET

WASHINGTON PLACE

PORTSMOUTH SQUARE

KEARNEY STREET